GREAT WESTERN STEAM – through the Cotswolds

GREAT WESTERN
STEAM
THROUGH THE COTSWOLDS

COLIN L. WILLIAMS

D. BRADFORD BARTON LIMITED

Frontispiece: 'Castle' Class No. 5083 *Bath Abbey* with the 12.55 Hereford-Paddington near Chipping Campden Tunnel on 18 October 1958. This fine locomotive, built in 1939, was one of those fitted for oil-burning in the immediate post-war years, and is seen in final condition with three-row superheater and mechanical lubricator, shortly before withdrawal in January 1959. [T. E. Williams]

Published by Enterprise Transport Books Ltd
3 Barnsway, Kings Langley, Hertfordshire WD4 9PW

Printed and bound in Great Britain by BPC Hazell Books Ltd

introduction

This volume takes the form of an out-and-back tour of ex-G.W.R. lines through the general region of the Cotswolds, which form a limestone upland area in the adjoining parts of Gloucestershire and Oxfordshire. A logical centre to commence, as this is a volume on railways, is Oxford, even though this is south of the Cotswolds proper; similarly too, Swindon is a fitting point to end this tour, being well off any limestone but still the end of the Gloucester-Kemble main line.

Apart from the long and fascinating single-line branch from near Oxford wandering through Witney to Fairford, the principal route followed is north on the Worcester line to Honeybourne, south-east to Cheltenham and Gloucester, thence back through the heart of the Cotswolds over Sapperton summit to Swindon. The first of these main lines, from Oxford to beyond Kingham, climbs gradually on the 'dip slope', then plunges down Chipping Campden bank to Honeybourne and the Vale of Evesham. The cross-country line thence through Winchcomb and Cheltenham to Gloucester follows the northern edge of the uplands. South of Gloucester, leaving the parallel ex-L.M.S. tracks to continue on towards Bristol, the G.W. pushed their line eastward up the Stroud valley, facing a severe climb to Sapperton on the 'escarpment', followed by an easy run down on to Swindon. This, it should be remembered, was once the route to and from South Wales—hilly and circuitous—as a result of the barrier of the Severn. This 'long way round', via Chepstow and Stroud, continued in steam days to be a useful relief route for Welsh traffic, for freights when the Severn Tunnel was near to capacity and for passenger services, principally on Sundays, when tunnel maintenance was under way.

Though this area of Western Region saw virtually every major locomotive class working in it or through it, one might describe it as 'Castle and 28xx' country—the former being typical on the principal Gloucester and Worcester passenger turns, and the latter most prevalent on the through freights.

'Castle' Class No. 7005 *Sir Edward Elgar* slows for the stop at Oxford in September 1958 with an up express from Worcester. The station here was rather unpretentious considering Oxford's importance as a railway route centre and its general business. In the late 1950s, for example, over 175 passenger and parcels trains called here in each 24 hours, of which rather more than two-thirds started or terminated at this point. With only one up and one down through platform, smart station working was called for and congestion was frequent, particularly with down trains.

[N. E. Preedy collection]

Summer Saturdays stretched the station capacity at Oxford to the limit, with a constant succession of passenger trains, many being extras from South coast resorts bound for the Midlands. Apart from traffic to and from the Midlands, these numerous cross-country services ran between places in the north as far apart as Newcastle and Birkenhead down to resorts ranging from Margate along to Weymouth; No. 6925 *Hackness Hall* waits to leave for Banbury with one of these from the latter in August 1964.   [D. M. Cox]

Adding to the congestion at Oxford was the fact that many of the trains calling here changed engines—particularly inter-Regional workings—or at least changed engine crews. Here No. 6855 *Saighton Grange* is about to be uncoupled from a Birkenhead-Bournemouth train on 22 June 1961. Replacing it for the run over Southern metals will be a 'West Country' Pacific. With the spacious and open layout of the station as shown here, it is difficult to realise that this once had an all-over roof (removed in 1890).

[R. H. Leslie]

A rather less commonplace scene at the north end of the station, in May 1950, with 'Bulldog' Class No. 3454 *Skylark* and an S.L.S. (Stephenson Locomotive Society) Special.
[Derek Cross]

Oxford would have been an intolerable operational bottleneck had it not possessed through roads, and as it was the four running lines through the station could barely cope with traffic at peak times. About 150 freights passed through each day in the up or down direction. 2-6-2T No. 4112 on a freight (above) is bound for Hinksey Yard, now the principal marshalling yard in the area. No. 5957 *Hutton Hall* beside the down platform, contrary to appearances, is on duty as station pilot. [J. R. Besley] Below, 61xx Class No. 6112 also heading for Hinksey with a train of cement hoppers. [D. M. Cox]

One could regularly see locomotives from all four Regions at Oxford and the ex-G.W. shed here (81F) played 'host' to a wide variety of motive power, ranging from Bulleid 'West Countries', ex-N.E. 'K3' Moguls, rebuilt 'Royal Scots', Stanier 8Fs and other types. In addition it had its own allocation of W.R. locomotives, amounting to 54 in 1950 and 64 a decade later. The shed lay north of the station and on the west side of the main lines. On 29 March 1963, No. 4093 *Dunster Castle* is backing out ready for duty after servicing.

[D. M. Cox]

A minor curiosity to be seen in and around Oxford in the last days of steam was 74xx Class Pannier No. 7412 with a chimney repaired in rather home-made style by the addition of what was said to be a portion of an oil drum—a repair probably carried out when a spark-arrester chimney had been taken off No. 7412. Here she is waiting for the board on the up through road, with a transfer freight from Yarnton to Hinksey in June 1962.

[J. R. Besley]

12

Scenes by Oxford station North box; above, No. 7905 *Fowey Hall* with the York-Bournemouth express, one of the two principal daily cross-country services which survived to the end of steam, and (below), 0-6-0PT No. 7445 picking her way through with a mixed freight.

[J. R. Besley]

Churchward Mogul No. 6309, standing in for the more usual 28xx rostered for this duty, heads north out of Oxford with a train of loaded petrol tank wagons from the depot at Thame.
[L. Waters]

No. 7013 *Bristol Castle* waiting to leave Oxford with a train for Worcester in May 1962. These were the heaviest W.R. engines seen at Oxford; 'Kings' were barred, although allowed south of Banbury to Didcot running light—usually when bound to or from Swindon. No. 7013 exchanged name and number plates with No. 4082 *Windsor Castle* in 1952 to enable a locomotive with the latter name to head the funeral train of the late King George VI. The original No. 4082, which the King had driven on one occasion, was in Swindon Works and could not be used.

[J. R. Besley]

No. 6927 *Lilford Hall,* in spotless condition, about to back on to a Bournemouth-York train for the next stage of the run north, May 1962. One of the Southern's 'Lord Nelson' Class, No. 30862 *Lord Collingwood,* had worked the express up to this point.   [J. R. Besley]

No. 6824 *Ashley Grange* leaving Oxford with the 5.15 p.m. semi-fast from Paddington to Worcester and Hereford, 13 July 1963. The Worcester line diverges from those to Banbury at Wolvercot Junction, just over two miles further north. [R. H. Leslie]

The Fairford branch left the main Worcester line at Witney Junction near Yarnton, four miles or so out of Oxford, and ran along the southern side of the Cotswolds to Witney and Fairford. Almost 22 miles long, this line was originally owned by a separate company and was taken into G.W.R. ownership in 1890. Here Collett 0-6-0 No. 2221 is leaving Eynsham with the 12.12 p.m. from Fairford on 23 May 1962. The last passenger train ran on the branch on 16 June following; chalked on the tender side are the words 'The End is Near'. [J. R. Besley]

Though it did not pass through particularly spectacular scenery, the Fairford branch was one of the most photogenic anywhere on the Great Western system and made an admirable subject for modelling. Witney, about seven miles from Yarnton, was the original terminus as well as the most important town along the branch. This scene, dating from the last few months of passenger services, shows the 'new' station at Witney, the former one having become the goods shed and yard; 0-6-0PT No. 3653, approaching from Oxford, will come to a halt by the column to take on water.

[J. R. Besley]

Outgoing parcels traffic at Witney was quite considerable—of locally manufactured blankets and gloves, etc.—and it became the practice for two or three bogie vans to be left during the day on the up road, leaving the down platform for use in both directions. Here, No. 7404 is attaching two parcels vans to the rear of the 6.0 p.m. from Fairford.

[J. R. Besley]

Handing over the token at Witney, with No. 3653 on a down train for Fairford. In the latter years of the branch in the 1950s, there were four passenger trains each way on week days, plus a morning out-and-back freight to Fairford and another parcels freight working as far as Witney.

[J. R. Besley]

More scenes at Witney; above, No. 9654 on an afternoon up train on the branch, a day or two before the last passenger train ran. Note the single line overbridge; east of Witney, these were built for a double-line, there being strong local hopes in the nineteenth century that this line would form part of a route through to Cheltenham. Below, No. 7404 waiting to attach loaded parcels vans to the 'up' evening train.

[J. R. Besley]   23

Lechlade, last stop before Fairford, with No. 7404 on the afternoon freight, 31 May 1962. The signalman is handing up the staff, before retiring to his diminutive box. Electric token was used from Yarnton to Brize Norton and electric train staff thence to Fairford.

[J. R. Besley]

A scene at Fairford (Goods) with a freight. This, the actual terminus of the branch, lay a short distance beyond Fairford passenger station, and had a goods shed, short platform, a small engine shed (a sub-shed to Oxford), and turntable. The latter was regularly used, as all locomotives on the passenger services ran chimney-first. 'Yellow' or 'uncoloured' classes only were allowed to use the line.

[J. R. Besley]

A last look at Fairford, and its passenger station, with 0-6-0 No. 2236 ready to leave for the return journey to Oxford with its two-coach set, 23 March 1957. One minor feature of the branch was that it possessed no distant signals anywhere along its length, full a.t.c. having been introduced in 1906.

[R. K. Taylor]

2-8-0 No. 3800 passes Walton Well Bridge north of Oxford with a freight for the Worcester line after a heavy snow fall in the winter of 1959. [L. Waters]

Principal railway cross-roads in the Cotswolds was Kingham, where the Oxford-Worcester main line, running approximately North-South, was crossed by the Banbury-Chipping Norton-Bourton-Cheltenham line, running more or less east-west. With four platforms and ample space for layout, it was—in pre-Beeching days—a locality full of interest for the railway enthusiast. 41xx Class 2-6-2T No. 4101 in May 1962 is waiting to leave with the 11.18 a.m. to Cheltenham. [J. R. Besley]

A further view of Bay Platform 3 and another 41xx, No. 4101, being given a final look-over by her driver prior to taking out the same Kingham-Cheltenham train. The lines to the right are to Chipping Norton; beyond the signal box can be seen the bridge carrying the direct Banbury-Cheltenham line opened in 1906

[J. R. Besley]

No. 4101, rounding the curve from Kingham up to join the Cheltenham lines, passes 0-6-0PT No. 9471 engaged in shunting in the sidings on the down side of the station. Passenger service ended in October 1962 but with occasional freight trains still serving Stow-on-the-Wold and Bourton-on-the-Water.

[J. R. Besley]

No. 4163 with the usual two coaches—alas, also virtually empty as usual—drawing across the main lines through Kingham from the bay platform on a Cheltenham train. The under-hung starter signals on Platform 1 were needed here to be visible below the platform awning.

[J. R. Besley]

The daily Worcester-Oxford pick-up freight, headed by 42xx Class No. 5205 entering Kingham, 23 May 1962. Below, No. 5205 setting back into the down sidings. On the right can be seen the sub-shed at Kingham, which housed the locomotive used on the Chipping Norton trains.   [J. R. Besley]

Her Kingham duties complete, No. 5205 prepares to depart for Oxford. Shedded at Worcester, this 2-8-0T is too worn out for any long distance work and is due to be condemned as soon as she needs any heavy repairs.

[J. R. Besley]

Little or no revenue-earning traffic has been available for 0-6-0PT No. 8491, seen arriving at Kingham with the pick-up freight from Cheltenham in June 1962.   [J. R. Besley]

No. 7031 *Cromwell's Castle* with the 12.05 p.m. from Hereford to Paddington draws to a
halt at Kingham. Worcester shed had a justifiable reputation for the fine condition of its
'Castles' right into the era when the 'Hymek' diesel-hydraulics replaced them.

[J. R. Besley]

2-6-2T No. 4101 on a
Kingham-Cheltenham train
draws away from
Stow-on-the-Wold
platform in the last few
months of service. This
station was the first after
leaving Kingham.

[J. R. Besley]

Bourton-on-the-Water, in
the heart of the Cotswolds,
with No. 4101 standing in
the loop to cross with
No. 5173 on a return
working back to Kingham
from Cheltenham, May 1962.
[J. R. Besley]

Conversation piece at
Bourton, with 2-6-2T
No. 5173 taking water during
a leisurely stop with the
10.50 a.m. ex-Cheltenham.
These lines through the
Cotswolds retained their
ex-G.W.R. 'flavour' right to
the end. [J. R. Besley]

No. 5173 again, leaving Bourton *en route* for Kingham. She was one of 22 51xx 'Prairies' withdrawn by the end of 1962.   [J. R. Besley]

Moreton-in-Marsh, 27 March 1964, with 61xx 2-6-2T No. 6147 shunting in the down sidings. This is the next station to Kingham on the main Worcester line.   [W. L. Underhay]

No. 4141 entering Bourton with a Kingham-Cheltenham train.   [J. R. Besley]

A striking study of one of Worcester's 'Castles', No. 7011 *Banbury Castle,* amid the woods near Chipping Campden with the 1.10 p.m. Worcester-Paddington, July 1962. [R. H. Leslie]

The other branch from Kingham was the one eastward through Chipping Norton to Banbury. A locomotive was normally housed in the shed at Kingham to work services on this stretch, varying from a 2301 Class 0-6-0 to a 41xx 'Prairie' in later years, or a B.R. Standard Mogul. Here, in May 1960, No. 4101 has charge of the branch train at Chipping Norton.
[G. F. Bannister]

Another view of No. 4101 and her two-coach set at Chipping Norton. This scene is full of interest for the modeller, even down to such details as the old horse-shoes nailed to the wooden beams of the cattle-dock in the foreground.   [G. F. Bannister]

'Modified Hall' No. 6989 *Wightwick Hall* slows down under the road bridge at the up end of Moreton-in-Marsh for the station stop with an up semi-fast from Worcester, 13 August 1957.   [T. E. Williams]

No. 4082 *Windsor Castle* (formerly No. 7013, renamed) with a clear road through Moreton on the 9.15 ex-Paddington, 28 May 1962. Below, the former Shipston Tramway branch left the main line at Moreton; an enthusiasts' special ran over this in April 1955, shortly before closure, behind veteran 2301 Class No. 2474.

[G. F. Bannister]

An up express, behind No. 7011 *Banbury Castle,* approaching the north portal of Campden tunnel, near the summit of the four mile climb faced by southbound trains from Honeybourne. This 1 in 100 bank carries the line up the steeper scarp slope on the north side of the Cotswolds; from the south the ascent is a long gradual climb for the thirty miles or so from Oxford.　　[J. R. Besley]

A cold morning in January 1964 and a threat of snow in the sky as No. 7002 *Devizes Castle* heads towards Paddington near Chipping Campden with a ten-coach express from Worcester.　　[Norman E. Preedy]

47

Overleaf: No. 5037 *Monmouth Castle* about to enter Campden Tunnel on a Paddington express, 9 October 1955. The portal is built of particularly massive local stone.　　[T. E. Williams]

Chipping Campden station is on a level mile or so of track at the summit of the bank; No. 7013 *Bristol Castle*, racing through on a down express, still carries a reporting number from an up working.   [J. R. Besley]

On an autumn morning in 1954, the four-cylinder beat of 'Castle' Class No. 5090 *Neath Abbey* disturbs the peace of the Cotswolds woods near Chipping Campden as she pounds up the 1 in 100. This train, the 9.50 a.m. ex-Hereford, was given the name of 'The Cathedrals Express' from the introduction of the Winter 1958-59 timetable.

[T. E. Williams]

A light seven-coach load for double-chimneyed 'Castle' Class No. 7007 *Great Western* in May 1962 passing Campden signal box and crossing. Her paintwork is, as usual, a credit to the cleaners on her home shed (85A) but she is leaking steam from one or more cylinder glands.

[J. R. Besley]

No. 4083 *Abbotsbury Castle* working all-out against the gradient up through the woods towards Campden summit, 16 April 1954. She is from Cardiff (Canton) shed and in a grimy condition that is in contrast to those of the class maintained in fine fettle by the Worcester staff.

[T. E. Williams]

Diesel railcar No. W10W has power off and begins to pick up speed rapidly as it heads down the 1 in 100 north of Chipping Campden on 7 July 1954, *en route* from Oxford to Worcester. This was Oxford's only railcar but Worcester maintained another six and they were at one time regularly seen on this route. Dating from the mid-1930s, and built by A.E.C./Gloucester C. & W. Co., W10W had two A.E.C. 'omnibus' engines with a total power output of 242 hp, 4-speed drive and seated 63 passengers. 1962 saw the end of these diesel railcars, their final sphere of operations being in and around Worcester; three have been preserved.

[T. E. Williams]

At Honeybourne one is down off the Cotswolds and beside the relatively flat Vale of Evesham and at this point the Oxford-Worcester line crosses the one from Cheltenham to Stratford. Seen here is an unidentified 'Hall' with an up Worcester-Paddington express, crossing over the lines to and from Cheltenham (in the foreground); 1 June 1957.

[T. E. Williams]

Birmingham-
Gloucester train,
hauled by 43xx Class
2-6-0 No. 9315 passing
the Honeybourne
'Intersection', June
1957. The '9300' batch
of Moguls, built 1932-4,
were the last twenty
of this numerous class,
with modified weight
distribution at the
front end to improve
riding at speed,
outside steam pipes
and a larger cab with
side-windows.
[T. E. Williams]

Scenes at Honey-
bourne, July 1962.
Above, 2-6-2T
No. 4113 alongside
the tiny coaling
platform and (below)
2-6-0 No. 7315
waiting for another
spell of banking duty
behind freights up
to Campden. Although
nominally classed as
a sub-shed (of
Worcester),
Honeybourne had no
actual building and
the single locomotive
allocated here was
stabled in the open.
[J. R. Besley]

A final look at
Campden bank, with
graceful Churchward
2-8-0 No. 2880, from
Southall shed,
competently handling
an up partly-fitted
train of vans, 1 June
1957.   [T. E. Williams]

With Mogul No. 6368 banking at the rear for the climb to Campden, No. 4999 *Gopsal Hall* starts off from Honeybourne with a freight on 1 June 1962. Most freights received banking assistance but piloting of passenger trains was rare, as loadings were usually kept within class limits for the 1 in 100.   [J. R. Besley]

Scenes at Honeybourne, June 1964; above, a down loose-coupled freight, hauled b
No. 6926 *Holkham Hall,* passes the signal box. Below, 41xx Class No. 4124 on a pick-u
freight and Collett 0-6-0 No. 2222 running 'light engine'.   [Derek Cross

No. 7902 *Easton Mascot Hall* at Cheltenham (Lansdown), 26 May 1958. This was the M.R./ L.M.S. station on the Bristol-Birmingham main line—a rather mean structure by the standards of the old Midland Railway, especially in a town with the architectural charms of Cheltenham.

[Norman E. Preedy]

Cheltenham Spa station (called St. James in the days of the G.W.R.) was the one nearest to the town centre and the main terminal within the town. Here No. 4101 waits to depart with a local in May 1962; on the left are the coaches of a train just arrived from Paddington.
[J. R. Besley]

Cheltenham (Malvern Road) was the station at the junction of the G.W.R. line to Honeybourne (and Birmingham) with the one continuing on to the terminus station at Cheltenham (St. James). No. 7026 *Tenby Castle* is seen taking the avoiding line past the station towards the latter, shortly before the closing of Malvern Road in the Beeching era. [Norman E. Preedy]

Last of the many 'Halls' was No. 7929 *Wyke Hall,* turned out from Swindon at the end of 1950, seen here near Churchdown, south of Cheltenham, on 21 November 1964. [Norman E. Preedy]

'The Cornishman', hauled by No. 7026 *Tenby Castle,* passing Elmbridge on the four-track section of main line between Cheltenham and Gloucester, October 1959. This busy section of line, used by both the L.M.S. and G.W., was quadrupled in 1942, at a date when war-time traffic was extremely heavy. For many years 'The Cornishman' was worked down from Wolverhampton to Bristol by a Stafford Road 'Castle', which then waited to take back the same express in the 'up' direction. [M. J. Jackson]

With the reporting number I V 53 chalked on the smokebox No. 5056 *Earl of Powis* heads towards Cheltenham on 29 August 1964. This train, a Saturdays-only Paignton-Wolverhampton, has been worked by the 'Castle' from Temple Meads. Most of the class had been withdrawn by this date but No. 5056, together with others from West Midlands sheds, had passed to L.M. Region ownership, which extended their life somewhat, following Regional boundary changes in the area in the late 1950s.

[Derek Cross]

'Granges' near Lansdown Junction at Cheltenham, August 1964; No. 6870 *Bodicote Grange* southbound with a fast freight bound for Severn Tunnel Junction and No. 6848 *Toddington Grange,* below, with a partly-fitted freight from Neath to Swansbourne.

[Derek Cross/P. J. Lynch]

For convenience of working, tank engines usually hauled the Cheltenham expresses to and from Gloucester, giving an opportunity for some smart running over this easy stretch of road even with lengthy trains. In July 1958, 2-6-2T No. 5105, with the ten coaches of a Cheltenham-Paddington express, is approaching Gloucester and heading for Central station. Here the train will be reserved, and worked out by a 'Castle'.

[T. E. Williams]

Gloucester Central, looking west; 2-8-0T No. 4254 clumping through with a freight o the up middle road in June 1956, and (below) 2-6-0 No. 4358 on a local train. A diese railcar and another Hereford local share the down platform, on the left.

[Norman E. Preedy/P. J. Shoesmith

'Castle' Class No. 5074 *Hampden* comfortably fills the 60ft. turntable on Gloucester shed (85B). Seen here in May 1960, this locomotive has been reboilered (with increased superheat) and fitted with mechanical lubrication but is without the 'nose-heavy' double chimney which spoiled the good looks of the 'Castles'. The latter feature was added to *Hampden* in 1961, three years before withdrawal. The last 'Castles' on Western Region remained active right to the final day of steam, working from Gloucester. [M. J. Jackson]

Swindon-Gloucester trains were regularly used as running-in turns for express classes after heavy overhaul at the works, as witness 'County' Class No. 1024 *County of Pembroke* near Standish Junction, on 3 July 1954. Behind the parcel vans at the rear of the train can be seen an upper quadrant signal, pulled off for a southbound train on the nearer ex-L.M.S.R. running lines. [T. E. Williams]

An assorted pair of Pannier tanks, Nos. 8491 and 8743, approaching Lansdown Junction with a Gloucester-Cheltenham train, 2 September 1961. The variety of motive power and trains along this section made it of particular interest to railway observers.

[T. E. Williams]

No. 7034 *Ince Castle*
getting away strongly past
Horton Road crossing
in November 1962 with an
express for Paddington.
[Norman E. Preedy]

The auto-train which shuttled between Gloucester and the outlying 'dormitory' villages in the Stroud Valley was normally composed of one saloon and a 14xx 0-4-2T but at busier times warranted a Prairie and two or three coaches. Here, No. 1453 on the 3.10 p.m. service to Chalford passes the level crossing at Horton Road on 4 April 1963.

[W. L. Underhay]

Shunting in progress by Tramway Junction with 0-6-0PT No. 4684 beneath an upper-quadrant gantry. Another Pannier and an L.M. Region Class 5 on the right are outside the ex-G.W. running shed just out of sight to the right. Freight traffic to and from Gloucester, as well as that through it between South Wales and the Midlands, was always heavy.

[Derek Cross]

Newly repainted 2-8-0 No. 3826 setting back wagons into the sidings at Stroud from a freight bound for Gloucester. Note the classic architectural style of the goods shed, built entirely of local dressed stone, with miniature flying buttresses and gothic-arched window openings. Beyond the sidings can be seen the wooded slopes of the Cotswolds.

[W. L. Underhay]

Another scene at Stroud, on 26 August 1963, with the up and down auto-services to the Valley passing. Quite surprising speeds were attained by these one-coach sets, particularly on the four-track section from Standish Junction into Gloucester where impromptu inter-Regional races were not uncommon on the parallel pairs of tracks.

[W. L. Underhay]

Most of the Stroud Valley auto-trains from Gloucester terminated at Chalford, a distance of about sixteen miles, but a few continued on to Kemble, up and over the Sapperton climb. No. 1451, waiting in the loop before starting her return journey, is seen on 9 June 1964, not long before the end of steam on this service. Chalford at one time had its own small shed (a sub to Gloucester) primarily to house a 14xx for the early morning workmen's Gloucester train. [Derek Cross]

No. 1472 and its saloon auto-trailer, after a smart bit of acceleration up the gradient, coast towards the stop at Chalford on a day in July 1963. At various of the quite numerous halts on this one-time busy service, the guard issued and collected tickets. [R. H. Leslie]

On a day of alternate sun and showers in August 1961, No. 7027 *Thornbury Castle* leaving Brimscombe with a Swindon-Cheltenham train. At this point in the densely wooded valley leading up to Sapperton, the gradient steepens to 1 in 74, and worse, for up trains; banking assistance is provided for most freights.

[Derek Cross]

An up goods behind No. 6952 *Kimberley Hall* crossing the nine-arch brick-built viaduct at Frampton Mansell, on the climb to Sapperton, 14 August 1961. Twenty wagons are within the unassisted **load** limit for a 69xx 'Hall' and she has come through Brimscombe without the need for a banker.

[Derek Cross]

No. 6918 *Sandon Hall* with a coal train passing the box by St. Mary's level crossing, banked in the rear by No. 7814 *Fringford Manor*. To reduce the amount of slow traffic through the Severn Tunnel, a number of freights to and from South Wales were routed via Gloucester despite the greater mileage involved.

[B. D. Coldwell]

For laden coal trains wrestling with the five mile climb up from Brimscombe—1 in 60 at its steepest point—the succession of curves did not make things easier. Here No. 3866, (last of the class) on the 1 in 75 below Chalford, has a clear fire and, like No. 6137 (seen above) helping her in the rear, has good Welsh coal burning in the box. [R. H. Leslie]

Another banking scene on Sapperton, with No. 3859 on an up goods on 18 October 1958, laying a trail of smoke and steam across the countryside. In the rear, visible only by its exhaust, is a 51xx Class 2-6-2T.

[P. J. Shoesmith]

Working heavy freights downhill on long stretches such as that from Sapperton Tunnel needed as much care on the part of enginemen as it did to surmount the uphill climb. Although No. 3840 had stopped to pin down some brakes in the normal way before beginning the descent, she still has traces of smoke and heat haze trailing from the brake blocks on her coupled wheels as she is pushed down through Chalford by her unfitted freight. At Brimscombe, a stop will be made to lift the wagon brakes for the gentler run down thereafter.

[R. H. Leslie]

In a break between spells of duty as banker from Brimscombe, 2-6-2T No. 6137 takes time off to re-position some wagons in the steeply inclined sidings in Chalford goods yard, July 1963.

[R. H. Leslie]

2-8-0T No. 4248 sends up a plume of smoke as she battles up the grade on 9 June 1962 with a train of Welsh coal. The top of this northwestern scarp-slope of the Cotswolds is about 650′ above sea level and the operational difficulties of surmounting the climb were some of the reasons behind the G.W.R.'s decision to tunnel under the Severn.

[Norman E. Preedy]

Summer sun on Sapperton; No. 3838 heads for home at Severn Tunnel Junction, with a through freight from Swindon, June 1962, seen near the entrance to the summit tunnel. 'Whistle frequently when passing through the tunnel' reads the board beyond the train, beside the up line.

[Norman E. Preedy]

No. 7023 *Penrice Castle* at speed with a down express in the cutting leading to Sapperton Tunnel. Just over a mile long, this latter is extremely wet in places and the 1 in 90 gradient up to the actual summit inside the eastern end can give footplatemen a nasty time with freight engines in poor condition.

[Norman E. Preedy]

0-4-2T No. 1472 again, suitably smartened up externally and with a head-board, at Kemble on 5 April 1964 on the occasion of a rail tour organised by the Gloucestershire Railway Society.

[Norman E. Preedy]

Scenes at Kemble
Junction; above,
No. 5065 *Newport
Castle* about to depart
with a Cheltenham-
Paddington train on
24 August 1957 and
(below) No. 5042
Winchester Castle
restarting another
similar train on 28
January 1959. Here, at
the southern edge of
the Gloucestershire
county boundary, there
were short branches in
pre-Beeching days—
west to Tetbury and
eastwards to
Cirencester.
    [H. H. Bleads/
    R. J. Leonard]

A scene at Swindon Town, on 26 May 1962, with an 0-6-0PT departing with a freight for Cirencester over the M. & S.W.J. line. This ran through Cricklade and Cirencester to join the Kingham-Cheltenham branch at Andoversford.   [J. R. Besley]

Auto-fitted 14xx Class 0-4-2T No. 5804 at Tetbury station after arrival on the 1.18 p.m. from Kemble, January 1959. A rail bus was introduced on this service the following month.
[R. J. Leonard]

One of ten or so of Swindon's local allocation of 45xx tanks, No. 4507, takes water in one of the bay roads at the station, 1 July 1952. [N. E. Preedy collection]

'Castle' Class No. 5048 *Earl of Devon* at Swindon's Platform 4 with a down train in July 1962, a month or so before being withdrawn from service and sold to a South Wales scrapyard. [Norman E. Preedy]

Another scene at Swindon, home of the G.W.R. and terminal point of this tour around the Cotswolds, with No. 2879 going well at the head of a mineral train.

[N. E. Preedy collection]